T0063316

A BOOK OF ROOMS

A BOOK OF ROOMS

Kobus Moolman

ISBN: 978-0-9870282-4-2
ebook ISBN: 978-1-928476-20-7

Deep South
contact@deepsouth.co.za
www.deepsouth.co.za

Distributed in South Africa by
University of KwaZulu-Natal Press
www.ukznpress.co.za

Distributed worldwide by
African Books Collective
PO Box 721, Oxford, OX1 9EN, UK
www.africanbookscollective.com/publishers/deep-south

Deep South acknowledges the financial assistance of
the National Arts Council for the production of this book

NATIONAL ARTS COUNCIL
OF SOUTH AFRICA

Production of this book was made possible in part
by a research grant from the University of KwaZulu-Natal,
under the auspices of the National Research Foundation

Text design and layout: Liz Gowans

Cover painting: Andries Gouws: 'Grahamstown residence
room with red curtains'. Oil on canvas.

For Julia

soli deo gloria

In memory of my father
Jacobus Philippus Moolman

Even if I have the help only of yellowing snapshots, a handful of eyewitness accounts and a few paltry documents to prop up my implausible memories, I have no alternative but to conjure up what for too many years I called the irrevocable: the things that were, the things that stopped, the things that were closed off – things that surely were and today are no longer, but things that also were so that I may still be.

– Georges Perec

Contents

1.

Who

2.

What

3.

Why

4.

When

1.

Who

The Room of Maybe

Black & white light. Dog-eared.

At the

back of a house in Greyling Street there is a room that comes in and out of focus

as he slowly moves his head There is another room before this one even – of this

he is certain – but it is so indistinct that only a small wooden bed with low sides

remains embedded in his memory Together with the smell of the brown shoe polish

(always Nugget) that his mother smears onto an old *lappie* at night and pins inside

his little vest to stop him coughing And the underwater sound of his own small voice

calling up to her from out of the drowned end of a dark passageway The room

(the back one) is a junk room, work room, sewing room before it becomes his bedroom

and much later that of his younger brother Because they argue all the time and

cannot share anything between them The room is rectangular and on its longest sides

directly opposite each other, there are two doors One door leads into the lounge where

he plays on the carpet with his plastic soldiers and his wooden blocks and his large

Buddy-L trucks (a cool-drink delivery truck, a flat-bed truck for carting sand or

wooden blocks, a cement mixer and a panel van with sliding doors) The other

door secured with a bolt and a padlock and with a black security gate on the outside leads straight into the back garden In the back garden there is a wash-line with five

wire strands, a swing with a cracked wooden seat, an old hibiscus tree, and further back

a large open area where his *oupa* has a vegetable patch with beans and potatoes and

mealies, and his father has three stunted orange trees, a large pile of second-hand bricks

encrusted with green mould, and a stack of rusted metal poles ('Cause you never

know when you might need them, his father always says) that attract fat spiders

There is also a third door in his bedroom On the same side as the one into the back

garden But in the opposite corner This door is never opened Across this door is

an old mahogany bed that his English mother bought in 1947 in Johannesburg He is

terrified of all the small things that crawl under this door at night and scuttle about

beneath his bed The bed is very high and when he kneels at the side at night to pray

(Our Father who art in Heaven forgive us our Trespasses) he presses down with his

forearms onto the mattress and lifts his knees high off the ground so the small

crawling things with feelers and claws cannot reach him There is a plastic under-sheet

to protect the mattress from the dreams that crawl up his trouser leg every night and

soak into his sleep, long after he should have outgrown the weakness There are

two large windows that look alternately onto the wash-line at the back (concreted into

the ground by his father to prevent rust 'Cause you got to look after what you got

he always says) and onto the *blinkblaar* hedge that runs all along the side of the house

(and is said to ward off lightning) and at Easter has small fleshy pink fruit that tastes

like absolutely nothing   There is absolutely nothing he can do except sink, and sink

deeper, and drown, when he wakes up at the back of the house in the dead of night

with long wet feelers crawling over his face and rough claws around his throat

pulling him down, down into the airless pit beneath his dreams.

The Room of Green

Fluorescents. Whine of small electric saw.

There are bookshelves

with thick manuals in editions of green and red and dark blue all the way round the room

There are large windows that cover two complete walls from the ceiling to just above

the bookshelves, with a view over the leafy part of the city and the uMsunduzi River

in the background There are old motor horns, shining wooden steering wheels

long-handled hand-brakes, head lamps with intricate metalwork and side- and rear-view

mirrors displayed on the walls, together with framed certificates confirming participation

in long-distance vintage car rallies There is a heavy imbuia desk with a bevelled glass

top and a black high-backed leather chair on wheels behind it There is a man with

a very big head and hands the size of a bunch of bananas and a voice so soft that

neither the boy nor his parents ever understand what he is saying The man always

wears a white safari suit with long white socks and white shoes Behind the man's desk

is a partitioned-off area with a high narrow examination bed covered in brown plastic

with a white sheet over the lower half which the boy is afraid to put his dirty boots

upon in case his father disapproves The partition doubles as a display case with

opaque glass on the outside, facing into the surgery, but clear on the inside It contains over a hundred toy cars of all makes and models   From small cement mixers and

break-down trucks to Willys MB US Army Jeeps and Model-T Fords (sedan or roadster)

His favourite, though, is the red and white Chevrolet El Camino convertible with fins

Because it looks as if it could swim underwater like a great white shark Because then

all the bigger boys at school (with names like Tasso and Vickus and Ferdie) would

leave him alone Just like that But sometimes when he visits with his father and his

mother he has to go through the small white door at the back of the surgery into the

kitchen where all the messy work is done   Like changing his bandages, cleaning

his dressings, removing his stitches, cutting off his old plaster casts with a small

electric circular saw or a large pair of silver cast scissors, and putting on a new one

all tight and wet and hot, and hardening clean and white in minutes On these

occasions a green plastic sheet is spread across the sink and his father lifts him up

and puts him down on top There is a window next to the sink and he looks out into

a small courtyard with a garden and a pond with stagnant green water while the

man with the big head and the big hands puts on a long green plastic apron and

tells him to sit still Very still Still as a stone holding its breath.

The Room of Growing

Bleached light. & swelling hands.

There are two doors

that lead, one outside onto the front stoep with its shiny red
polish, the other into

his sister's bedroom directly behind him There is a long crack in the
wall that opens and

closes depending on the weather There is a wide window with
long green blinds

made out of something that snaps sharply like bubble-wrap if he
bends one of them

The window faces straight onto Greyling Street, which runs left to
right and back again

all day and all night Even on Sundays Even when he is not there
When he is at church

in his little blue safari suit staring up into nowhere, or at school
sitting behind his

scratched desk with his eyes squeezed tight in case the teacher
asks him to read

out loud from their comprehension book about Carol and Roy
who go to the corner

café for their mother, like good children, and buy milk in glass
bottles with shiny

aluminium tops and unsliced Oxenham's white bread in a brown
paper packet

Through the wide window he watches his father drive off every
Friday night in his

brown Ford Cortina XLE (Big 6) with blinds in the back window
And he wonders

where his father goes And why his mother does not go with And
why sometimes he

wishes his father did not ever come back There is a wooden floor
with a small hole in

one plank through which he tries to push his soft penis one night in imitation of some-

thing he knows not what   There is a high ceiling made of long boards like the floor

but slotted into each other in the tongue-and-groove fashion   The ceiling is painted white

and it is flaking in parts and in other parts there are brown stains from the leaking

corrugated iron roof   There is a heavy old wardrobe in dark imbuia that used to

belong to his *oupa*   In fact long before the room was the boy's it belonged to his *oupa*

before he passed away in the old Grey's Hospital with his empty blue eyes staring up

into nowhere   The wardrobe has a long narrow mirror in the door in the centre and deep

pockets of camphor-scented darkness on the inside   The mirror is flanked by a simple

S-shape carved in light relief into the wavy grain   There are also two identical second-

hand pine beds   One for himself   And the other for his much younger brother

Before he moved to the back room   Because they argue all the time and cannot

share anything   There are two patchwork duvets made by their mother from scraps of

barefoot shame and old shirts, dresses, curtains and pillow slips   There is a pine desk

under the window that he has no choice but to share with his brother, although he

prefers doing his schoolwork on his bed with his back against the cracked wall and his

cold feet sticking out over the other side   (In this position he writes a long poem

which his mother copies out in her best handwriting and frames

---

19

about a race of men

with eyes all over their body instead of skin and plastic flippers where their feet should

be) There is a small shortwave transistor radio that plays his favourite programmes

like *Jet Jungle* and *High Adventure* and *Squad Cars* 'They prowl the empty streets at

night, waiting in fast cars, on foot, living with crime and violence' There is also a

bookshelf made by his father from off-cuts scrounged from the factory workshop

and fixed to the wall above the head of his bed for his growing collection of *The Hardy*

Boys and Willard Price Later it will include Louis L'Amour and Edge and Sven Hassel

and the poems of Rod McKuen (with black and white pictures of couples wearing bell-

bottoms walking hand in hand on the beach while a big white sun sets behind them)

There is a small tin that he hides amongst the spare batteries, the brylcreem and hankies

the cans of deodorant and nebuliser masks, the dirty bandages and tubes of Betadine

ointment, in the two top drawers of the desk *His* drawers Unlike the bottom drawers

which belong to his brother and are always empty Except for the one occasion when

they were full of Crunchies and Chocolate Logs and packets of Simba chips (Cheese &

Onion and Plain) which his brother stole from Van's Hoek Kafee (at his instigation, though)

and for which his gullible brother was thrashed with a strap by their father in the garage

over and over While he (because he has a hole in his heart, as his mother screamed when it came to his turn, when his father went to fetch him from where he was hiding

under the green bench in the lounge) got off (as he always did) with just a warning

(and a smile) from his mother The tin in his top drawer is a flat rectangular Strepsils

tin with a lid held in place by a broad elastic band The tin holds all the luck he needs

to stay upright in assembly with his eyes squeezed tight during the Our Father Forgive

us our Trespasses In case he should fall over or wet himself It goes everywhere

with him Like his hands Like his concave chest Like his memories of blonde

six-year-old Bunty who lived just across the road before the security branch

policeman moved in with his wife and her short crimplene skirts There is the sound

of traffic all day up and down, and people on the pavement outside his window and

black delivery men on bicycles And then a siren goes off somewhere and his

father comes home from the factory for lunch smelling of cocoa beans And afterwards

his father has ten minutes in his high wing-backed chair in the lounge, and suddenly

everything in the house is very still and dark and the boy is underwater again

Under the water where he can hold his breath longer than his brother (who has no

talents to speak of, except being impressionable) Longer than anyone else in the

whole world in fact And he hears the sound of guttural voices knocking against the

low step into his room from the polished front stoep And unknown

---

things that

happen in rustles behind the locked door into his sister's lilac room The door that

locks from her side only Things he spies through the keyhole of the bathroom door

Holding his breath so that she does not hear him Until everything begins to swim

around him And inside him And inside him someone shouts and shouts sharply

And he turns and he runs and he runs out into the back garden Past the garage

Far away into the night that smells of orange blossom and the mint under the leaking

tap and the yesterday-today-and-tomorrow bush and rotting figs that have fallen to the ground.

The Room of Family Holidays

Bright sunlight. Fat smell of frying.

There is a long

window with thick metal burglar bars painted white The window runs the length

of the room and looks out across the deep blue Indian ocean on the south coast of

Natal It is a long narrow room with three single beds One bed is perpendicular to the

room, in the middle, with its head against the back wall facing the ocean (This bed is

reserved for his sister) A second bed is directly underneath the window, and horizontal

to it, at the far end of the room The third bed is in the same position but up against

the back wall The second bed is a source of continual dispute between himself and

his brother Because both boys always want to sleep right by the window so they can

be the first to see the ocean and to see the sun come up This dispute is finally solved

by their father (with the help of his strap) who decides that they must take turns to be

at the window on their annual Christmas holidays Although this still does not prevent

them arguing over who slept there last and whose turn it is this time About to go

into his final year at high school he feels that such squabbles are below him, and he

magnanimously allows his brother access to the bed by the window without any

argument, and with only a superior smile He feels that he is on the brink of something very significant in his life, something almost adult And though he will perhaps feel

this same overwhelming power again For example when he buys his first car, a 1982

white VW Jetta Mk1, or when he publishes his first – and only – piece of writing, a

rhyming poem on Mother's Day in a consumer tabloid distributed free from local Spar

supermarkets It will never be with the same absolute confidence in his ability to get

what he wants And what he wants now is to find a way to talk to the long-legged blonde

girl who stays in the big cottage at the top of the road, with its own private access

to the beach via a long flight of steps made from old railway sleepers And so he

doubles up on the arm and chest and leg exercises he does with his expander springs

(the thick ones with the blue handles, not the red ones which are too easy) Even

though his mother warns him not to strain himself And he swims in the surf directly

in front of her house even at high tide (when his mother warns him not to because of

his weak legs and the strong undertow) And he tans himself at low tide on the flat

black rocks in full view of her pathway So that she has no choice but to notice him

And when she smiles at him on the third day and says hello how are you on the fourth

he knows with a certainty as firm as the black rocks that he is chosen And that

he will always get what he wants Just by willing it And on the fifth day she invites

him to her house and into her small bedroom (with a big blue teddy bear on the bed)

and together they listen to a stretched tape of the Beatles' *Sergeant Pepper's Lonely*

Hearts Club Band (I'd love to turn you on) And on New Year's Eve they walk hand

in hand as the white sun sets behind them, along the beach to a party on the wet sand

where he drinks *Spook en Diesel* (just like his father's policemen friends) out of a

polystyrene cup and the blonde girl is asked to dance by an older boy, a university student

he assumes, because of his long hair, who comes to the party in a red beach buggy

with a surf board tied to the top, and who makes the girl laugh by whispering something

in her ear And he (the boy with a hole in his heart, at the heart of this story) feels everything

crumble and slide away beneath his small feet in their differently-sized orthopaedic boots

And he leaves without saying anything to the girl And stumbles home along the cold

moonless beach He knows that if he goes home now his mother will want to know

What's wrong? What happened? Are you alright? And she will want to kiss it all

better (As she always does) But he is much too old for all of that stuff now So he

hunches behind a dune smelling of damp vegetation and rotten fish-bait and dog turds

and he sniffs his right hand repeatedly, the hand that held onto hers (and smells of

coconut oil and Simba Puffs) and he licks it and puts it inside his trousers and he waits

until it is midnight and the fire-crackers have died down and he can open their back door and creep into the sleeping house And in the morning his mother spoils their

whole family by frying bacon and eggs for breakfast (sunny-side up) with white toast

This is a special treat Just for holidays she says smiling at him Because apart from

his father who eats *mielie pap* every morning for breakfast everyone else always

has Pronutro, regular or chocolate flavoured, with milk and no sugar And that is

that Finish *en klaar* That is the morning when he learns how much easier it always is to pretend than to admit a painful truth.

·

The Room of Rural Teaching

Hot glare. Cicadas.

There is nowhere

to hide anything inside a room without any corners, where everything happens

in a language without him anywhere in it There is a worn stable door painted green

on the outside but left bare on the interior There are two small windows in wooden

frames directly opposite each other that cannot open There is a floor made of cow

dung and blood, and polished black so that it shines and is perilously slippery

There is a dusty thatched roof that hides spiders and beetles and who knows what

other feverish things that whisper and breed and multiply in the dark, the way that

dependency upon others does There is a vertiginous mix of emotions inside him

Excitement that he is finally out of his parent's home and can do what he wants for

the first time in his life Pride that he is helping those less fortunate than himself

And fear that they will murder him in his sleep There is a second-hand pine wardrobe

with a broken lock that still holds the sweet sandalwood smell of the discount shop

in Indian town where his father bought it Before all the injections and tablets and

ointments When he still drove and would haggle for everything The wardrobe has

three drawers One for socks, one for stained underpants, and the third one for some-

thing else, like the habit he keeps in a 1-litre plastic ice cream container, together
with a packet of Rizla papers and some mix (Stuyvesant Blue) and a jumbo box of Lion
safety matches containing a minimum of 235 standard size matchsticks When he
leaves the farm the wardrobe stays behind as a fumbling form of expiation for failed
promises There is a nest made by hornets in the dry wall opposite the stable door, that
he destroys as soon as he moves in and adds to his long list of things to feel guilty
about for the rest of his life (Like Bunty and his compliant little brother and the big
bruises on his mother's arms from his rough boots when she carried him about
like a baby, long after he was not) But nothing and none of that matters anymore Not
at all Because he will always find something or somebody else to take the blame Because
just like holding his breath, it is the one thing he excels at There is an overgrown patch
of spinach and pumpkins across the dirt yard And beyond that there are acacia trees
with thorns as long as his fingers, and aloes, and further off a valley with steep rocky
sides There are pitch-black nights without the hint of a moon when, for the first
time in his life, he feels what it is like to be truly alone (All those long many moments
on his own in the cold prep room before going in to theatre do not count because he had
been only part conscious) With only his two rough hands to console him and the
sound of goats rubbing themselves against the rough outside

wall of his room There

are horribly thin dogs that howl on the rocky hillside behind him in the middle of the

night and haunt his animal dreams with their wet longing There is an enamel potty with

rust on the handle that he keeps under his bed and empties early in the morning in

the veld before anyone else is up, when the mist lies like cobwebs on all the bushes

The bed is the same pine bed he slept on as a child, except now it has a new foam

mattress (courtesy of his father who argued it into the deal over the second-hand

wardrobe with the small Indian salesman) There is no bookshelf but a large copy of

Die Tweetalige Woordeboek / Bilingual Dictionary and Afrikaans for Standard 7 lies

on top of his pine desk The desk, like the old bed, he knows from earlier circumstances

Although he doesn't have to share it with anyone else now The desk sits under one

of the small windows, the window on the right (facing the stable door) From there

he watches terrified as the clouds climb up over the edge of the horizon and swell

and change colour until the entire sky is hard and heavy with their disapproval

There is nowhere to hide then or run away to, as he could when he was a child, and

the only way he survives is to pray to God (Forgive us our Trespasses) that the

lightning finds someone more deserving of punishment than himself He does not

deserve the kindness of his hosts who carry in to his room every night an old metal bath (which they prop up with bricks) and five litres of lukewarm muddy water in a

rusted oil drum they had heated over an open fire He does not take account of how

far the youngest daughter walks every day with her squeaking wheelbarrow and her

plastic drum to fetch water for him from the Ngwenya river Since there are no taps

in her home Or that she is only thirteen when she bends over the old bath in her black

school gymslip revealing a dirty pair of pink panties, to scoop out his dirty water

(Which her whole family would have used for a day) He takes for granted everything

that he sees, that he feels or tastes Even the ability of his hands and his legs to think

and to move on their own So much so in fact that when one day inside him something

speaks sharply in the voice of his father and says he will lose it all one day, everything

even his ability to speak and to move on his own, if he does it again, if his hands

carry on . . . he does nothing Does what he always does Nothing except turn and run

(he who always comes last running) into the moonless night breathless and heaving

hands stained and sticky with hallucinations, his eyes swimming straining, straining

like hungry dogs against the hot rope of their longing.

The Room of What He Excels At

Everything spinning.

There is a smoky

room with a stuffed buffalo head on the wall outside the entrance to the men's toilet

stinking of urine and stomach gases, where dirty water lies on the floor and crude cocks

are scrawled behind the cubicle door   There are blacked-out windows, a pool table

with heavy legs, and a television set in the corner without sound playing soft porn

with Swedish subtitles (Ja! Ja! Ja!) There are a hundred excuses and explanations

justifications and mitigations that he makes for failing to meet everyone's expectations

In the spinning room with signatures and photos on the sticky walls of South African

musicians like Lance James and Jeremy Taylor ('Ag pleez Deddy!') and heavyweight

boxing champions like Mike Schutte and Gerrie Coetzee   The room where he

always arrives breathless and heaving, his shirt-front wet with sweat Long after everyone else has left.

2.

What

The Room of Impressions and First Appearances

Grey & drizzling.
With one new character.
On red high heels.

He is wearing

a cream polo-neck jersey with a white vest underneath, a pair of black chinos that his

mother lengthened by letting out the turn-up, old grey school socks, and his favourite

brown Harris tweed jacket that belonged to his grandpa (the father of his mother, not

oupa, his father's father) who bought it in Jo'burg after the war when he came back

from up-North and the only job he could get was as a barman at the Observatory

Golf Club, earning two-and-six for a twelve-hour shift with one day off a week She

is wearing Pure Silk by Lenthéric, with her short black hair in a bob just like his mother

The jacket is his favourite because it makes him look older than he really is and

serious, and because coming back in the bus from the National Schools Festival in

his matric year, the girl with the red hair, who had a boyfriend waiting for her at home

the girl who had shown him how to kiss with an open mouth and a wet tongue (his friends

called it French-kissing), had said that all the writers she had seen in pictures (and other

intense people like security branch policemen) always wore jackets like that

There are three precise rows of white plastic chairs with precisely ten chairs in each row

There is a long trestle table at the back of the room covered with a long white cloth that

hangs to the floor There is an urn on the table and three neat rows of cups and saucers

a stack of small side plates with yellow serviettes and two unmatched dinner

plates with Tennis biscuits and stale Romany Creams (mint flavour) that he stuffs

into his mouth two at a time during interval (in case they are finished before he can

return for seconds) and then chokes on Just like he did at that wedding reception at

the Lions River Country Club when he was ten, when he vomited all over himself, and

everyone thought it was because he had eaten too many stuffed eggs, when really he

had choked on the marble he had been sucking in his mouth (his lucky smokie) that his

mother always warned him not to There is a Steinway grand piano in the front of

the room with its shining top propped open and beside it three upright chairs without

arms One for the cellist at the end furthest from the piano, and two for the violinists

first and second There are large French doors with a view onto a day without any sky

or sun or colour and only a lonely *Piet-my-vrou* calling And in the doorway he stands

aside to let her pass The way his mother taught him And she smiles and lowers

her eyes The way her experience with other men taught her And he pays for their

tickets The way his father hated doing for anything without haggling first or

wheedling for a discount And all the while he wonders why he accepted her invitation

to come all the way out on a cold grey day to a cold sandstone house in Greytown

to listen to the chamber music of Ernst Bloch Actually he does not mind Classical

music But then it must be popular classics like Tchaikovsky's *1812 Overture* (with

real cannons) or *Bolero*, which he used to listen to over and over again in the lounge

as a child until his father grew so sick and tired of it he scratched the record with a long

nail Just like that In front of him Finish *en klaar* Finally he concludes that

perhaps he accepted her invitation because she is so much older than him (thirteen

years he finds out later) and a divorcee Which makes him feel grown-up for the first

time in his life And that someone is treating him as a grown-up For the first time

in his life But it might also be because she smokes long cigarettes and wears designer

dresses and high heels like an actress in one of those slow and serious movies (the

black and white kind with subtitles he can never read quickly enough or work out

who is saying what But where all the men wear tweed jackets) He cannot dismiss

the fact that it may even be because, with her long neck and her small head and strong

legs, she reminds him of a praying mantis (She studied as a dancer, before snapping

a tendon and becoming a nurse instead, he finds out later) And though mantises terrify

him (he had read in one of those Did You Know questions on the inside of a yellow

Chappies bubble-gum which he had twisted his brother's arm to steal for him, that

the female devours the male after mating) he is the first to admit their mysterious power

The power to decipher in the old air everything that ordinary people only find in

the *Reader's Digest* and the *Huisgenoot* or the twelve o'clock re-broadcasts of 'The Bold and the Beautiful'.

The Room of Independence

Incense. & candle-light.
Same long shadows from childhood.

There is a wide

window with pale green curtains, facing onto Burger Street and the provincial offices

of the Department of Transport There are two doors that lead, one outside onto the front

stoep with its cracked and broken red tiles, the other into a long and dark passage with

a dusty wooden floor and a dead light bulb that is never replaced There is the same

old pine desk with four drawers filled with unopened NBS bank statements and old

school exercise books he had bought because the girl with the red hair, who had a

boyfriend waiting for her at home, had told him that all real writers keep notebooks

for their profound thoughts and ideas But since he had never had any profound thoughts

and ideas (or the discipline to be still and listen for them) the books are still sealed

in their brown paper wrapping In the drawers there are also dry Bic pens (only black)

blunt pencils (Rexel HB) and dog-eared photographs and love letters on perfumed

paper from all the girls who could not love him the way he wanted with their lips and

their hands But who wanted to be his friend instead (This is how he first learned the

terrible meaning of the word 'platonic', a word he had thought previously referred to

a small planet) There is the same narrow pine bed he had slept on as a child With

the same old patchwork duvet he had dreamed beneath (of feelers and claws and

sticky wet things) so many long years ago in Greyling Street where his parents still

live (although his father is struggling with the side effects of his Lupron injections for

prostate cancer At eighty-one he is too old for surgery) And where he goes every Sunday

afternoon for lunch, and takes his dirty linen to his mother who washes and irons

it for him and returns it in a neatly folded pile with a Tupperware *bakkie* of frozen mince

on top or chicken stew or *melkkos* in winter, which he eats sitting on his single bed

with his back against the wall and the door closed, out of sight of his housemate (so that

he does not feel guilty for still being Mommy's Big Boy) with a book open beside him

(Stephen King or Douglas Adams) Perhaps even the local newspaper, *The Natal*

Witness, which he gets free because he works there now, just around the corner in

Longmarket Street as a nightshift sub-editor The days are short and the nights are long

and difficult, and he gets cramps in his stomach and headaches because he does not

fit in with the other subs and journalists who talk about sex and parties and politics all

the time and wear gaudy T-shirts with slogans on them like 'End Conscription Now'

and 'Troops out of the Townships' Although he cannot admit it to his colleagues, it is a

source of deep shame for him that he was never accepted to do military service because of his weak chest and unmatched feet and his heart with a hole in it Because above

all else he wants to be a man and do real manly things with his hands and his feet like

kicking and punching and slapping hard, the way his father did with his brother and

his sister and his mother, and then his brother again (because the little bugger has no

mind of his own and always does exactly what his older brother tells him) and even

Fluffy, their little fox terrier too   Because straight after school when all his friends had

gone away on long noisy trains to learn how to strip and clean and shoot an R1 rifle

and how to march up and down *Aaaaandag*! *Eentweedrie Eentweedrie* in their

big brown boots and hard *staaldak* he had been forced to take the only job that did

not require any technical skills, and for which he did not need a qualification: teaching

Afrikaans to black children at a farm school Even though six months later he was

back home with his pine bed and his desk (but not the wardrobe) because the job had been

too demanding for his back and his feet and his heart with a hole in it Or so he had

told everyone And his mother had said See I told you so No one ever listens to me

But so what he tells himself now when the sky gets hard and heavy with disapproval

(Father forgive us our Trespasses) There are many places to hide little secrets and habits

in a room with four corners and a pine wardrobe and a bookshelf with a masonite back

and a firm belief that because he was chosen at birth not to be the same as everyone else

he cannot be subject to the same rules as them   And so after midnight when his

shift is done and everybody in the street is fast asleep he opens the curtains

and opens the windows and sits still as a stone in his darkened room and stares out

And then, while his stained fingers are busy, the night, the merciful night with

quiet eyes quietly takes off her shiny top, the one with a hundred little silver sequins

and underneath she is wearing absolutely nothing   And he inhales deeply and he

holds it all in, and suddenly everything begins to swim inside him And on New Year's Eve

when everybody in the street is dancing and drinking and singing 'Shuld auld acquaintance

be forgot', when he is alone, with only his hands to console him and his secrets and his

consoling old lies, an orange 1973 VW Passat stops in the driveway and the woman

with the designer dresses and Courtleigh cigarettes (in the red box) knocks at the door

on the front stoep   And it does not surprise him at all that underneath her velvet

coat (with Arctic fox fur at the collar and around the cuffs) she is wearing nothing at all

Only her pale skin, only her soft pale skin overflowing with something he has never

felt before in anybody's eyes   Not even the eyes of the girl with the red hair   Not even

his mother's   Something that trembles like the appetite of a size eleven scalpel blade

And he believes that he is on the brink of something very significant in his life

Something almost adult But then suddenly her face begins to melt and her hands

shrivel into her arms and her arms shrink into her shoulders and in a flash she slithers

across the red tiles into the dark bushes at the edge of his hunger And he is alone again

And there is a rusted anchor in his chest And he cannot breathe No matter how wide

open he opens his mouth And the sharp voices that speak sharply in the pit of

his stomach, in the voice of his father, saying he will lose it all everything, one day

even his hands and his sneaking eyes if he ever . . . even once more . . .

The voices will not be silenced No No Not Not by anything.

The Room of Wordlessness

Curtains around the prone shape of hands.

There is the smell

of undiluted Dettol that he remembers And ammonia and old vomit, fresh paint

(Double Velvet – Velvaglo) and wet sea-sand A smell that swells and recedes as his father

slowly moves his head There is the sensation of claustrophobia smooth aluminium

surfaces, shining needles, clear PVC tubes and sharp sea-spray There is the thin

sound of wind far-away in the dark hollow of a shell whispering There is the gargle

of sounds in a hollow language in a putrid mouth without a hint of his father anywhere

in it There is nowhere for him to look without seeing the thin body of someone

who used to be his father before his father gave up being anyone and expected everyone

suddenly to feel sorry for him There is the white uniform of a bed that carries a weightless

cargo from one reluctant breath to the next There is nothing to be said by anyone

standing staring or sitting around the high bed staring at nothing So nothing is said Nothing at all Just like that Only the waiting.

The Room of the First Time

Take the weight on your forearms. She says.
Slowly. Keep the momentum. Yes. Yes.
Don't worry if it doesn't happen the first time.

There is

There is a small pencil triangle (upside down) with a dot in the middle, in the top

left-hand corner of a journal (not a Moleskine, which is too costly, but the Croxley

JD6235 with 128 lined pages and every page empty except for the pencil triangle) that

records the date at the grateful age of twenty-seven years, three months and fourteen

days, when, in a cramped bedroom that smells of hair spray, old make-up and cigarette

smoke, in her mother's second-floor flat overlooking the Oribi airport, he finally

at long last, leaves his long childhood behind There is a large cross in black ink

through the pencil triangle (upside down) with a dot in the middle in the top left-hand

corner of a journal (the Croxley JD6235 with 128 lined pages and every page empty

except for the cross through the pencil triangle) that records the eventual death of his

father from renal failure in a small room that smells of plaster and paint and old vomit

in the brand new state-of-the-art Grey's Hospital on the hill, on the night when no-one

in the whole wide world knows where the hell to find him When at long last, finally

his hands taste and touch and see everything in the whole world they have always wanted.

The first time.
It was over so suddenly
he wondered. What's all the fuss about?
But that did not stop him coming back the next night.
For more.

The Room of White

Faster.

There is a pan-handle

gravel driveway leading up to a small cottage that the woman in designer dresses rents

after moving out from her mother's cramped second-floor flat with its view of

skydivers sliding off the steep pitch of the sky There is a small stoep with a white

plastic garden table and two plastic white chairs There is a front door with no handle

and only a heavy brass knocker he must grip firmly to pull the door closed behind him

There is a short passage with a bare wooden floor and an antique hallstand that she

inherited from her father who was master of the Natal Supreme Court from 1962 until

his sudden death from a brain haemorrhage in 1980 in the parking lot of the court

just as he was about to get into his brand-new V-6 Ford Granada which he had only

bought a week before There is a white king-sized bed with a red bolster pillow and three

round red cushions in damask silk Everything else in the room is white The walls

and the door, the floor and the ceiling, the bookshelf and wardrobe Even the light that

comes in through the white sash window There is a glass figurine of a dancer by René

Lalique on top of the white bookshelf There is a framed print by Claude Monet against

the white wall of a woman in a white dress walking through a field of red flowers

———

On the bookshelf are titles he has never heard of before   That he is afraid are perhaps

not Christian Titles such as *The Tao te Ching, The I-Ching* and *The Tibetan Book of*

the Dead There is also a large format full-colour manual with the Latin names of all

the secret and scary things that do not belong to his body Things like the *mons veneris*

and the *vestibule* Or things that do belong to his body like the *frenulum*, but that

mean something completely different in fact The way that bleeding does now And

through the white sash window one morning he sees the ghost of his father with wide

open eyes swimming up the long driveway, searching for him like a bird with its long beak

because other people are living at his old flat in Burger Street where his father's ghost

went to apologize for everything he had not done And for everything that he had

And like a reflex he ducks and he hides Because the ghost would not approve of him

sharing a table and a bathroom and a white king-sized bed with an older woman and

divorcee, *nogal*, who smokes and who knows the Latin names of all the secret and

scary things that belong to his body The body he was left with at birth after there was

nothing else left to fill up the blank spaces The body he has always been ashamed

of because it cannot be trusted to stay upright or dry Even though deep down he knows

it is futile to hide Because his father always said that if he could change his job and finally at long last, be someone, anyone in life other than a storeman in a chocolate factory, then he would be a detective.

The Room of Promises

Water. Birds. Stone.

There is

a tall blue sky without any railings He remembers He remembers the woman saying

Marry me With this body I thee worship Within this place of basalt and sandstone

we shall make the nesting place for our souls There is a sun-tanned wind with

strong legs Catch me! Catch me he says (And he hears, but he also does not hear

himself using the same voice he used as a child, when he stood naked and wet and

small on the green plank across the end of the bath and threw himself into his

mother's smiling arms) Look, look at me I am flying! And the swallows celebrate

with their quick wings And the cliffs ring with their singing And the loud voices he

remembers from all of his past, and their long shadows too, are overwhelmed by water

A clear water welling up from out of the black rocks.

The Room of the Dream

Except for a very strange
green light. & even stranger sound effects.

But then

there are . . . Suddenly there are . . . eyes with heavy footsteps
that follow him wherever

he takes off his feet From out of nowhere there are eyes with
heavy footsteps that

run without resting or even needing to breathe through all of the
liquid nights he dreams

of sleeping beneath And in his sleep a man appears with no eyes
in his head With

eyes all over the soles of his feet instead, and his feet as large as
a loaf of unsliced

white bread in a brown paper packet from Van's Hoek Kafee at
the corner of Boom

and Oxford street The man looks like someone who visits dreams
all the time, every

day, even those dreams that are not remembered Those that
shine like the sun with

singing and flying and falling that is forever, not downhill This
man, the man with

feet large as loaves of unsliced bread, is everything the dreamer
is not, but at the same

time too, everything the dreamer dreams of being And the man
with the big feet is

carrying an extraordinarily big bundle of lies, and wherever he
stops, he lays a lie

down that immediately springs up fertile and tall behind him And
this way the man

moves and this way too he grows lighter and larger as he moves
and sheds the lies

he carries Until his sack is empty And his hands are empty But that does not matter

now because now he is as large as a mountain And the dreamer is overwhelmed suddenly

by the weight of everything around him, which is the weight of the hole in his heart

and of all the expectations he expects her to have and that he is afraid he will never

never in all of his life be able to satisfy And he forces himself awake He sits on

the edge of the king-sized bed, holding his heart in his shaking hands And the whole

world suddenly feels so small and so distant and frail he is afraid to stand up in case

his two clumsy feet break something and his father finds out, and finds out it was not

his young brother at all (This is why for so many long years long after he could actually

walk on his own, his mother always carried him everywhere) Everything is white

all around him, as ash, as ice Even the thin night that comes in through the white

sash window And he turns to look at her, concealed in stillness beside him, she, the

woman transformed into a legal term now (official as husband and spouse or homeowner

words that previously he had assumed would attach themselves like caravans to the

ends of other people only) And everything lopsided and clumsy inside him, everything

he had hoped would disappear or at least change beyond recognition, once he

had entered and come out on the other side of her, the woman with the long legs and

long white cigarettes, everything small and crawling with feelers and claws inside him

everything suddenly swells with ice, hard as ice and disapproving
And a shadow close

and compact as his mother's arms rears up suddenly between
him and the woman in

the bed And he cannot see over or under or around or through it
Where are the birds?

he cries out   Where are the birds? But no sound comes out
Where are the wings of the birds to take him up and over?

The Room of More

Shhh. She says. Shhh.
Just be still. She says.
Hold me. Hold me. Like this. She says.
Let us just sleep. Just sleep together.
Haven't you had enough? Enough.
But his hands cannot.
& ever. Stop.
& his hunger will not & ever. Let go.
Wanting & wanting. To want.
Enough. She says. Enough!
Stop it! Stop!
You're hurting me.

The Room of Free-Falling, Forever, Not Downhill

1-2-3. 1-2-3. 1-2-3.
1-2-3. 1-2-3.
1-2-3.

There is the Odd

Fellow's Hall at the top of Longmarket Street, near the railway station and Dove's

Funeral Parlour There are twisted paper streamers strung across the dusty ceiling and

coloured balloons that hang from the lights and the old fans There is a raised stage

at one end of the hall covered by a heavy maroon curtain There are screaming children

who run across the front part of the stage, between the curtain and the edge, and

leap off Then run up the short steps at either end of the stage screaming still, and

leap off again and return and repeat the whole thing Until their parents intervene

At the other end of the hall, directly opposite the stage, is a long row of steel trestle

tables covered with red cloths that reach half-way to the ground On the tables are

glasses and bottles and bowls and plates and cups and cutlery trays of stuffed eggs

spicy meat balls and little pointed sandwiches, cold chicken drumsticks and wings

sausage rolls and small samoosas There is a row of fold-up armless wooden chairs

with slatted backs all the way round the perimeter of the old hall And here he sits

(the one at the heart of this story, with a hole in his heart) with his arms folded tightly

---

across his chest and his legs closed and crossed at the feet like a sulking child Like

a child holding on to the hand-hold of its hurt And he refuses to look at the dancers

in shining outfits and coloured smiles, sweeping and spinning around the room like

coloured tops (As a child his plain wood top never spun upright like the other boys'

So he gave up and played Dingbat instead with a green Sprite paddle But then

the elastic snapped and his father refused to get him another one Do you think money

grows on trees hey?) And he sits still as ice instead, with his arms folded and his legs

closed and crossed at the feet, and he stares at the dusty parquet floor The floor is

scratched and scuffed There are drops of black paint in some parts, even the rusted

head of a drawing pin stuck into the wood In other parts some of the small rectangular

wooden blocks are missing And as he stares at the dirty gaps left in the parquet floor

by the missing wooden blocks filled with dust and dirt and hair something dark stirs

within him, something far away in the dark turns and raises its dark head and looks

him full in the face, something magnified, with feelers and claws whose patchwork

cover has been torn away And suddenly he is a child again, in the early icy morning

and his parents have locked their bedroom door He is a child playing on the dusty

carpet in the lounge with his green plastic soldiers and his farm animals, his wooden

blocks and his Buddy-L trucks (the cool-drink delivery truck, the flat-bed truck for

carting sand or wooden blocks, the cement mixer and the panel
van with sliding doors)

and he is building a tower to reach all the way to the topmost icy
peak of the sky

Like the new all-glass Capital Tower on the corner of Berg and
Church street, with

designer dress shops and a Chinese restaurant and a cinema
on the second floor

where years later he takes a young Dutch nurse he met while in
Grey's Hospital having

an infected ulcer on the ball of his left foot debrided and irrigated
and whose name goes

right out of his mind as he stands in the hot glare of the cinema's
foyer lights and has

to introduce her to a former classmate they happen to meet On
the top of his wooden

tower he will place a small glazed ceramic figurine called Doc
who always wears

a white safari suit with long white socks and white shoes, and
who is missing the front

part of his base so that he stands always with his feet poised on
the edge of the void

From the top of his tall new wooden tower Doc will be able to hear
everything wet

and whimpering, sloshing like a mop in a bucket of water, in the
locked world below

And to build this tower the little boy will first put two blocks down
flat onto the

carpet (Fortunately the carpet is not fluffy, otherwise his design
would not work)

The blocks are laid horizontally, one above the other just less
than the length of a

block in-between After that he puts two other blocks (also flat)
across the first two

length-wise, joining them in a square of sorts On top of these again he will lay two

more, at the bottom and at the top, directly parallel to the ones below And so on

And so on Turn after turn Slowly Whimpering and sloshing, the blocks alternate – now

on top, now underneath, left and right – as the tower grows Until it is up to the boy's

waist when he stands dizzy with something like vertigo now, and there are only four

blocks left in the blue barrel that contains all of his soldiers and his cars and his plastic

farm animals The tower shakes slightly as he holds his breath hands sticky with

hallucinations, and he prepares to place Doc on the platform he has made at the top

out of the last four blocks in the barrel The tower trembles and he flinches as if before

a blow, and the grimace on his face already has the shadow of a fat hand But Doc

does not react Doc is not afraid of who dances with who quick or slow close or not

whimpering and moaning, whispering slippery wet words all the while Like the surfer

in the red beach buggy who seduced the girl with the blonde hair and the long legs

on the beach that night when everything fell suddenly through the boy's fingers like

burning sand and he was left alone Because Doc is not afraid to stand alone at the

top of the tower with all the churning world below staring up at him pointing and

sniggering Because Doc can fly Even from the top, so close to the peak of the sky

when the boy suddenly for no reason pushes the tower over Just to see what will happen

(The same way he did when he promised blonde six-year-old Bunty she could have

his old plaster cast when it came off if she put his lucky smokie into her tiny *koekie*

and kept it there for a whole game of hide and seek amongst the bushes in the back

garden Just to see what would happen) Just to hear the crashing of a hundred small

wooden blocks down into a broken heap Just to feel the soft wings of Doc, like a

moth, a brown moth, brush against his skin A glazed moth under the lamp of the

moonlight As the little ceramic man swims unscathed out of the sulphurous flames and the retribution.

The Room of Self-Pity
(allegro)

Because

*What? Because They all fall down Because There is a hole
Where his heart Where his nerves*

*Where his breath is meant to be Because When he was twelve
When they all played spin-the-bottle*

*Because Because he wants to know What if? What like?
What? Because he missed out Because*

*When the bottle pointed at him, & the girl with the short
mousey hair who had spun it, took him around*

*the side of the house where it was dark & narrow & his heart
was beating fast because she was going to kiss him*

*Because that was the rules Because everyone else did But
she said no No She did not want to Because*

*Because he has a hole where his heart Where his nerves His
mouth is meant to be & she laughed & she*

*made him promise, promise to pretend, pretend to everyone
else that she had kissed him*

With a soft mouth

*and with closed eyes, like everyone else Because that was the
rules Because when they came back*

*all the other girls were giggling Because they knew They knew
That the girl with the short mousey hair*

*had not kissed him That he had never been kissed before
Because What? Because they all Because he always falls
down Because.*

3.

Why

The Room of This is Not It, No, This is Not It at All

Broken smell. Something like promises.

There is a floor
There is a door
There is a roof
There is a ceiling
There is a bed
There is a wardrobe
There is a window
That starts at one end and goes all the way to the other
That opens and shuts at will when left alone
That covers only the essentials and leaves big dripping holes for his eyes to blow through
That is in-between this and that So as to prevent everything else falling in
Where he discovers just how much appetite he really has in the reddest part of his heart
Where he prefers to keep the door closed
That wants to see what is on the other side
Because
Just because.

The Room of Going Nowhere

Crawling around his cold. Cracked mouth.

There are once more

two doors that he remembers And again they lead out of a room
with a white king-

sized bed into another place with a different shape But with the
same sour air

The first of the doors that he remembers (directly opposite the
king-sized bed with

the red bolster pillow and cushions he recognises from other
circumstances) leads

into a narrow passage with the same antique hallstand (the one
his wife inherited after

her father's death from a sudden brain haemorrhage) that had
stood in the entrance-

way of the cottage, and a heavy kist in Burmese teak that her
mother brought with her

when she was forced to move in with them Because she kept
going astray between

her bathroom and the bedroom, and leaving her front door wide-
open as a wallet the

whole night long The second of the two doors that comes back
to him is adjacent to the

king-sized bed which he makes every morning with a sheet and
blankets and a bedspread

Unlike the patchwork duvet which he had used for so many years
and now lies folded up

with mothballs in a black bin bag on top of his *oupa*'s old
wardrobe in the front

room in Greyling Street, where his mother still lives, thin and
alone as a ghost

gnawed hollow from the inside by everything she had done for
him and everything

she had never done for his younger brother But you never know what lies around the

corner, his father had always said So she has put her name down on the waiting list at

Sunnyside Retirement Home for a single room with frail care and one main meal per day

The second door leads into another room Her (not his mother's) dressing room and

walk-in wardrobe that smells of cigarette smoke and make-up and musty shadows, where

the 40-watt bulb burns all day because the thick white drapes are never opened

(You never know who might be watching, she says) Impaled on the high-pitched

voice of his father's ghost (Who left the light on hey? How many bladdy times must I

tell you to turn the light off when you leave a room?) he turns off every single switch

in the house, including the kettle and the stove, the radio and television and microwave

Even if he leaves a room for a few seconds Even if someone else is still there

In her dressing room there are hanging racks with tops and dresses, jackets and

pants, skirts, scarves, cardigans and belts All carefully hung by colour, with the

palest items at one end – the whites and the greys and silver – moving through

to the darkest – the deep blues and purples, and finally the black items at

the other Everything has its own white plastic coat hanger and a clear plastic sleeve

to protect it from the dust and the dirt And on the wooden floor underneath each item

is a matching pair of shoes Some with high heels and some low some open or

closed, and even boots, full or half, with zips or laces In the room with the shape of

a room that contains a king-sized bed, there are (once more) two windows The first

window, long and narrow, runs across the top of the wall behind the bed, just below

the ceiling This window is too high to see anything out of except a strip of distant blue

with clouds that pass occasionally across and swell and change colour until the entire

sky is hard and heavy with their disapproval There is nowhere to hide then or run away

to as he could when he was a child (Father forgive us our –) And the only way he

survives is to pretend The second window in the room that has the shape of a room

that pretends to forget, is directly opposite the door that leads into her dressing room

where the light burns all day This window looks onto the front stoep painted grey

with white wooden pillars, and onto the small garden beyond enclosed by a high

concrete wall with spikes, so he cannot see the street and only hears its drawn-out

guttural complaint In the garden there is a large Leopard tree that the previous owner

(a single man with a young child) had planted for its shade, and a wiry Bottlebrush that

she bought from McDonald's Nursery when they moved in (to stamp the impression

of her personality upon their first property), and which he waters with a monotonous

sprinkler during the day when she is at the hospital (he still works the night-shift at *The*

Natal Witness) leaving him alone all day long with her monotonous old mother in her

blue-rinsed hair and her knee-high stockings, who is stuck on the same question all day

long like a long-playing record with an itch it cannot reach What is the date? What

is the date? What is – ? On the other side of the concrete wall covered by a cat's

claw creeper, through a dark wooden door that always sticks are the big old Jacaranda

trees, the uneven pavement slabs, the muddy verges slippery with squashed purple

flowers and the deep and wide litter-filled gutters of Boom Street Parallel to Greyling

Street, the street he was born and grew up in, Boom Street is the same street he walked

along so many long years ago in his little blue safari suit en route to the bus stop to

catch the 9am City / Stad bus on a Saturday, to take him to the library for another

book of myths about creatures with eyes all over their body instead of skin and

stranger things that happened although they could not ever have Or in his little black

cap and his blazer and his striped red and black tie on his way to Model Infants' Primary

school, the first school he ever attended (Unlike his brother and sister he did not go

to crèche because his mother was worried he would not cope going to the bathroom

without her) The same school whose orange-tiled roof he can see from his front stoep

sticking out above the concrete wall with spikes, a hundred metres down the road

But on the opposite side It is no longer used as a school, having been given to the

provincial department of Social Welfare because of its large grounds where old

people can queue for their old-age and disability pensions and child support grants

And yet in summer, when the air is gorged with the sound of lawnmowers and the

smell of newly-mown lawn, then he imagines that he sees the old lollipop man in his

white coat standing at the side of the road ready to rescue the little children from their

sticky toffee dreams (This was one of the many odd jobs his grandpa had when

he was boarded from the South African Railways for chronic emphysema When

the specialists said he only had six months to live And he went on for six more years

In a single room at the Jan Richter Centre with a bed and a built-in cupboard) And he

imagines too that he is winning the dressing-up race on Sports Day (The only race

he ever has won And only because his favourite game at home was to dress up in his

sister's clothes So he knows how to do up buckles and belts and zips and press-studs

and how to slide-shuffle in his mother's shoes that fit over his unmatched black boots

Stop that You're stretching my good shoes she would always scold But with a smile)

And if he is very still, still as a stone, and he closes his eyes and makes a secret motion

with his hands, like a traffic officer in white gloves, then he can also imagine that he

is alone in the girls' cold bathroom with the cold tile floor and the large white washbasins

(Because he wants to know what it looks like inside and whether it smells of the same

sour secrets as the boys') And then suddenly the headmistress Mrs Richardson, enters

with her bouffant hairdo and her long red nails and bright red mouth And inside

him somebody shouts and shouts sharply with the voice of his father And he runs

And he trips And he scrabbles past Mrs Richardson into the blinding corridor

that smells of crushed Jacaranda blossoms and sudden afternoon storms and

floor polish (in the red tin with the spiky yellow sun coming up like a welt).

Unable to run further.

Only his feet stop.

But. The rest of him. Keeps moving.

The Room of In One Place

Still. Still.

There is a chair now

that sits in a small square room with white walls and a dim fluorescent light

And does not do anything Or go anywhere Or speak even There is a chair that sits

in a corner with its faded arms on either side and its old legs closed and crossed

at the feet There is a chair that waits for something to happen that is not the same as

the thing that is happening the same all the time around it, day in and day out, slowly

and in minute detail There is a chair that sits in a corner and whines to all the old

ghosts through its clenched teeth and its small grinding fists that the best, oh yes, oh

yes, yes, the best is still to come Mark my words.

The Room of In One Place (cont.)

aka

The Room of Nothing Happened

Still.

There is a chair now

that sits in a corner of a small square room And sits precisely where he always does

It is a high wing-backed chair with floral upholstery, faded as a scar and thin from

wear and from where he has sat for so long speechless in one position The chair

has a repetitive rocking action But because it is squashed into a corner its motion is

restricted to static jerks, like small repeated shocks, that over the years have gouged

two holes into the corner of the walls behind it, exposing the grey concrete and the

thinness of his heels There is a white masonite door directly opposite the chair

that leads into a dining room with mottled grey floor tiles and a heavy antique table

with carved ball-and-claw legs where no-one ever sits down to eat preferring to eat off

their laps instead in the lounge in front of the loud television (a 32-inch Sanyo), so

that no-one ever needs to open or move their mouths to do anything except chew

and swallow and chew again There is a window beside the chair (on the right) that

looks onto the overgrown backyard of their neighbours, a sullen old couple who have

lived in the same house ever since he was a child, walking the long uneven road to

school in his black cap with its red *krans* aloe badge and a little leather satchel over

his hunched shoulders Always walking in the same way, with his arms stretched out

stiff like a tightrope walker, to balance himself across the uneven pavement slabs and

the little driveway bridges And always in exactly the same direction too

Out of his green front gate with the number 82 on a small wooden block in the middle

then turning right and proceeding up Greyling street for about two hundred uneven

paving slabs Past fat Mrs Adcock with her black 1955 Vauxhall Velox that stands

unused after her husband dropped dead one day in the driveway from an aneurism

Past his friend Yuri who trades marbles with him and has a large terrifying grey goose

called Smokie Past red-faced Mr Hitchcock whose maid goes every afternoon to the

off-sales at the Polo Tavern at the end of the road to buy him two Castle quarts for the

night Until he comes to Oxford street Then turning right and walking for about one

hundred slabs past his friend Jacques who has no father, but who can draw brumbies

and pumas and whose mother works at the Polo Tavern at night Until he comes to

Van's Hoek Kafee at the corner of Oxford and Boom streets (the dirty little store he

twists his brother's arm to steal stuff from) then turning left and walking under

the old outstretched branches of the Jacaranda trees, past the same house he lives in now (Who lived there then? he wonders Did they too stand like him on the little

stoep and stare at the world going by and stare at the ageing sky and wonder why the

distant past was always so much more real than the present?) Walking until he

comes to the crossing in the road where the lollipop man waits in his white coat to take

him across for another day of pinching and teasing and beating by the bigger boys (with

names like Tasso and Vickus and Ferdie) In the small square room there is also his

old pine desk under the window, and sometimes he sees the brown-haired daughter

of the old couple next door when she visits on weekends with her two squabbling sons

And as he watches her bend over the little plastic pool in the back garden in her black

skirt and low-cut top, something buried inside him stirs slowly and flashes its hungry

eyes toward the floating surface But he looks away from that frozen gaze And the

woman straightens up and flicks her mousey-brown hair out of her mouth and yawns

with her wide-open pink lips And he is safe again On even ground again Because

– next to holding his breath, and finding somebody else to take the blame – this is one

thing he is still good at, spying on the world through his fingers and pretending he

has a right to Because their bedroom door was locked And he could not sleep Because

of the noise of mops in his dreams Because nothing would have happened long ago

in that room without any corners, that room where there always was too much to hide

Nothing would have happened if that little girl, bending over the bath in her little

school gymslip, had not straightened up Had not turned around And seen And seen

what his one hand was doing And he would have been able to forget Or at least

pretend nothing had happened Because nothing had Nothing He told them all so

in that meeting in the principal's office with the large table with fluted edges and a

bevelled glass top Because one day soon when he leaves *The Natal Witness*, editing

the Market Indices and Property Guide and What's On for the Week Ahead with a table

of sullen night subs, he will sit down at his old pine desk (with its four drawers and

scratched yellow top) and he will unwrap one of his Croxley JD6235 exercise books

(with 128 lined pages) and open it at the first page And in his spidery handwriting he will

put down the whole story of what happened and what did not and what never would The

whole story while it is all still so clear While it keeps coming back Clear as a syringe

and as the fluid inside he needs to keep on remembering, to keep on coming back to

the whole story From the black and white rocking horse on the front stoep with handles

on either side of its head and the purple plastic helmet he wore when he rode his

tricycle up and down the driveway pretending to be Jody Scheckter To the rough feel of

the masonite placemats and pot stands his father had made for the kitchen table

And he will write down too (He will He will There is still hope It is the only thing still

left in the bottom drawer of his old pine desk) He will write down everything that comes

in to him through his eyes and his ears and passes out through his hands as he

sits still as a stone and spies on the world through his stained fingers Everything

From the taste of his favourite smokie after it has been inside Bunty for a whole

game of hide and seek in the back garden And the shadow of a fist that falls across

his wife's face like a heavy muscle one night in her sleep To her mother's monotonous

low mumbling outside their locked bedroom door What is the date? What is the date?

What is – And in his remembering, and in the putting down on paper of all of

his memories, in the remembering of them there (not for others – there is too much

for which there are still no words in his vocabulary – but for the words themselves

So that they may lie beside each other and softly touch and make up) he will undo the

knot that had cut off the light to his heart at birth And he will kick it loose from him

like a swallow shedding air as it climbs the sky Higher Higher But then suddenly

the mousey-haired daughter of the old couple becomes aware of someone watching

her and she slaps her arms across her wide-open breasts and snaps around and stares

straight in his direction And he thinks she recognises him and that she remembers the

hardness of his lips and the hunger of his hands and his teeth

75

as he kissed her that

night around the side of her house When they all played spin-the-bottle When he tried

to force her mouth open Stop! Stop! And to force his tongue inside You hurting me

Just like he had seen his father do with Auntie Audrey (who was not really his auntie

just a good friend of his mother's) on New Year's Eve in the cold dark garage smelling

of engine oil and concrete And like a reflex he ducks back inside the high wing-backed

chair with floral upholstery, faded as the surgical scars on his legs and his chest and

thin from wear and from where he has sat in one position speechless as an eye

and watering For almost all of his life Just pretending.

The Room of What is on the Other Side

He only wants to know. The size. & the shape.
Of her areolas.

There is a weightless

night without the suspicion of a moon There is a weightless night with lying tracks that

cannot be lifted once they have been laid across his heart There are furtive shadows

of plane trees that twist in and out of the long wind like lies There are the thin faded

front seats of a 1982 VW Jetta Mk1 with a black long-handled hand-brake raised

between them in front of the old cricket nets in Alexandra Park behind the run-down

pavilion and the ruins of the Chinoiserie-style bandstand that was demolished by a tree

in the Christmas day floods in 1995 and never repaired There is the steamed-up front

windscreen that faces the uMsunduzi River and a faceless and pale king-sized bed with

a bloodless bolster pillow and three empty round cushions in damask silk There

is a bloodless deal to open her fat legs and let him in in exchange for a Taxi-Two KFC

Special and a mini loaf (with gravy) on the side There is the smell of stale sweat and

talcum powder and vaseline that remains on his fingers and on the faded front seats

long afterwards Long after he has forgotten her name and the small animal sounds she makes as she sucks him like a bone.

& on.
& more.

The Room of Spillage

*What is the date? What is
the date? What?*

It all comes

back to him It keeps on coming The back-to-front image of his
mother burning like

a negative Back-to-front and intimate as a negative headless
with white skin all over

her body All over white as a negative And him on his bare knees
On his knees in front

of a small black keyhole When she is whiter than anything he
has ever seen or dreamed

When he wakes up at the back of a house in the dead of night
with clammy fingers around

his breath, dragging him away from somewhere with him in it to
somewhere where he

is not Where there is only the smell of engine oil and cold and
darkness Where there

is no explanation for the sudden hot dryness in his bones that
swallows all of his

voices and his ability to move on his own without handles Where
there are a hundred

excuses, explanations, justifications and mitigations that he
makes for snatching an old

woman by the wrist one morning after work when he is desperate
to sleep And wrenching

her away from the bedroom door and shaking and shaking her
until she stops her

questions And dragging her through the cold dining room and
shoving her back

into her own floral wing-backed chair in the windowless lounge.

He cannot. Feel.
The end of his skin. Any longer.
But still his hands.
Will not. Stop.

The Room of Repetition

Dragging.
Everything hot & sticky.

And then

there is room 302 on the seventh floor of the Albany Grove Hotel opposite the City Hall

in the middle of Commercial Road There is a man at the window with a hole in his

pump, holding on to the blood in his hands to prevent himself leaking all over the

carpet While the early morning pigeons and raucous mynah birds throw themselves

off the ledges of the tall buildings about There is a small woman with a freckled face

and a flat chest, and her wedding ring in the bedside drawer washing his monotony

out of herself in the small bathroom with the flickering light On off On off Like

the monotonous beacon in the black bay beyond that all night long over and again

tried to drown something that had lost all feeling in its skin Until he can feel no longer And never again.

The Room of Afterwards

He tries. To pick up his feet.
Quickly. Quick. Before the other guests wake up.
But his eyes spill. Every whole thing.

There is

with every step he takes, a feeling that he does not know what the outcome will be

Whether his feet will find the wooden floor Or not Whether the floor will even hold

him up There is, with every step he takes in the direction of his eyes, with every day

he swallows, tasteless and hard as the one before, a feeling that all forward movement

in his life has stopped and that he is slowly rolling backwards And the chance he

might once have had to do something about it went by several years ago But he is

good at pretending not to notice It is almost second nature Not noticing the heaviness

in his breath The static in his muscles all day and night The weight upon his tongue

And, besides, he does almost like feeling sorry for himself It is at least some kind of

compensation For feeling that something more vital than muscle and nerves was left

out of his machinery at birth And so it is that in the early morning in the icy early

morning there is just a boneless echo left in the bathroom mirror under the flickering

light when the hotel maid comes to change the sheets and towels and to empty the

sanitary bin An echo that drags its slow sound up the hill back home Fatal as a hospital.

The Room of What is Left

Less. & less.

There is just

a long crack left in the wall that opens and closes depending on
the weather

There is just a wide window with broken green blinds that faces
straight onto the

past, that runs left to right and back again all day and night every
day Even when

he is not there There is just a bare wooden floor with a hole in
the middle through which

suddenly everything drops There is just his mother, musty as a
wet towel, on her

knees in her blue crimplene dress thinner than a ghost, sweeping
up the fragments of

fifty years in the same leaking house, and packing the pieces into
a cardboard box and

closing the lid and taping it shut and never opening it again Not
even when she gets

to the other side To the Green Wing that smells of urine and
stale photographs

There is just his wooden rocking horse Just a long green couch he
always hid beneath

to escape from his father A chiming clock that only worked if it
hung skew Just a

formica kitchen table with five matching stools (bought by his
father at discount

because the sixth one was missing) A glass display case keeping
the faded reflections

of smiling faces (The way the eyes of the dead keep for all of
eternity the last thing

they ever saw Or so his mother believed) Just a brown stain in
the centre of the

---

garage floor where something that could not ever be mopped up or replaced leaked out

and ran a long time ago There is just a blue Ford XR3 that sat unused in the dark

garage after his father's death Because his mother never learnt to drive Because his

father would not let her learn in his car (What if you bump it hey?) Because no-one ever

wanted to go into the garage afterwards After the darkness moved in It is too dark

there his mother said It smells he said Of oil and concrete and darkness without any

breath Like falling from a cold height And lastly The very last piece his mother

sweeps up and packs away into the cardboard box, is the hefty block of his father's

voice faraway at the bottom of her watery eyes That is it That is all The rest of her

life she puts out onto the pavement And leaves there And by the morning the whole lot is gone Every last drop Just like that.

The Room of And Just This Once More

Tongue inside his.
Two cracked.
Hands.

And then there

is him And then there is her (with a hint of fine hair around the areole of her nipples)

Plus the other one (The one who chews gum all the time) And they are tangled in a

sticky slippery sloppy knot on the white king-sized bed with the red bolster pillow

and three round cushions in damask silk Then there is the low monotonous mumbling

(What is the date? What is the date? What – !) outside the locked bedroom door of an

old woman with blue-rinsed hair who leaves the bathroom door wide-open like legs

whenever she goes There is his small uncircumcised penis flaccid and slow as a slug

Allopeas Gracilis The common garden variety with no shell or body parts or blood

pressure in its responses ever again There is the brittle sound of collapsing A thousand

wooden blocks all in a heap There are photographs of broken skin and bruises and big

red welts all the way up the old woman's arms and around her neck too, her thin

skin wrinkled as an old fowl's There are no excuses There are accusations, implications

and denunciations instead There are signed dated and stamped forms in triplicate

instead, in the matter between the plaintiff and the defendant initialled on every page in his precarious scrawl, and spread out across an official-sounding table with

fluted edges and a bevelled glass top that for all of eternity keeps the reflection of that

moment burnt like a negative, white-hot as a negative in the acid of his blood There

is the flailing sound of collapse, all in a heap, as the small ceramic figurine falls Through

his hands Through the deep air And its neck snaps.

The Room of the Last Dream

On all sides. Steepness.

There is

There is a voice somewhere far away underwater that remembers a nightmare she once

had (the one who once once upon a time was a wife, when wife was a word he still

could remember) when she fell asleep under the wisteria bush with her head in his

lap and his two hands and the ten fingers on his hands dragging themselves back and

forwards and from side to side through and through her short black hair and across

her pale soft skin When she woke herself up whimpering like a dog, whimpering like

a dog on a chain because of what she had dreamed A dog with a hole right through

its heart With a chain right around its neck With its neck dragging around a

concrete yard back and forwards and from side to side, all day long Until it choked.

4.

When

The Room of Something Suspended
(sotto voce)

No sound No No movement No None at all Because It keeps
It all Keeps coming

Back & back To him What? What is that? There A garden?
With cracked scents

& dripping Things with feelers Feet with boots That bite
Brown shoe polish Inside

his little chest His favourite smokie Inside her little koekie &
concrete The taste

of oil On his eyes The smell Of falling Without any bottom
Shhh Shhh No sound

No No movement No Because Because It keeps Keeps coming
Back & back &

back To him The garden With claws Hands with feelers Eyes
& fingers & fingers

that smell Cold & darkness His favourite Yes Keyhole In his
mouth On his knees

Yes Still as a stone Holding Who art in heaven Father His
breath Her skin

Forgive us Her White as a negative When He suddenly White-
hot As a negative

& wet all over Like a mop Jerks the door open You little
fucking pervert! I'll teach you to spy on your mother and me!

The Room of That Last Time

Sshhhh

It comes

It all comes Back to him There where he is now In his faded chair Still Staring

at nowhere Where he is also not where he is Where it all comes Back The oily cold

And air Dangling from concrete A small wooden bench made by his grandpa (the father

of his mother not oupa, his father's father) from a World War 2 packing crate in Egypt

In the stores In Tobruk, where he was a store-man The small wooden bench With

a hole in the middle On the top Through which he tried to push his small penis one night

in imitation of something he had seen Over and again On his knees The small

wooden bench lying on its side And the smell The smell of faeces running down

white legs Turning slowly On his brother's brown school shoes with black laces

broken at the ends where the little plastic seal had come off His brother's brown shoes

scuffed on the soles from being dragged all the way through the dust and over the

stones of his short life towards that other small room where he was kept overnight

That last time Buried in the deep end of a dark passageway Until his father came to

fetch him And to take him To the garage That last time After the security guard

at OK Bazaars (the one in Church Street where there is a charismatic church now

Father Father forgive me) caught him stuffing comic books down the front of his trousers

(*Kid Colt*, The Fastest Gun Alive, and *Tessa*, with her long blonde hair and her white bikini

and Rocco de Wet, *Die Grensvegter*) That last time In the dark garage that smelled

of oil and concrete and something invisible Like oxygen Or pressure Or regret

That once released, no matter how long ago, far away and shrinking, is too large ever to be reversed.

The Room of Folding Up the Cold

There are.

There are

only two holes left in the cold of the small square room where the high wing-backed

chair with faded floral upholstery once sat, arms tied on either side and two thin legs

with varicose veins closed at the clamp and choking There is no light left at the end

of the day for the washing of all the eyes he has used up There is with every breath

with every step he takes in the direction of the cold wind, the feeling that he is

walking across old mattresses Or empty water The feeling that he is breathing through

a sheet of ice That he is seeing from a long way off And that is all That is it That

is all there is left for him to pack into a cardboard box and fold closed Left flap first

then top, followed by the right, and finally, at long last, the bottom which he bends

carefully at the corner and pushes underneath the first flap Just like that Finish *en klaar.*

Cold.

The Room of And How Now

Cold.

There are
There are
only certain indelible questions that remain in the room that has
the smell and the shape of a room that cannot forget

How does he still stay upright? After crawling

How does he stop himself leaking away into the red earth? After
leaking away

How does he still walk straight? After bending

How does he stop himself falling over when the earth tilts? After
falling over

How does he keep looking up? After looking the other way

How does he stop himself feeling that all feeling for him has
ended where his skin begins?

How does he?

Yes Yes

How does he do any of it? Afterward

Anymore.

The Room of Hunger

In all of his. Everywhere.

Where it is

It is as if the old kitchen has no linoleum floor As if the ceiling is not white rhino boards

As if the old walls have no shelves built into them for rows of antique cups and saucers

pink and pale blue with flower motifs, roses and geraniums and small yellow daisies

It is as if the kitchen table with the streaked grey formica top and the four black metal

legs and the four low stools covered in grey plastic are not all bending slowly under

the weight of something invisible Like time Or regret As if he is not back there Not

opening the old drawer with the broken metal handle Not taking out the masonite

placemats that his father had made from off-cuts scrounged from the factory workshop

As if he is not setting out the placemats on the cold table Two on one side (his father

with his sister) and one on its own For himself And the other at the head of the table

For his mother So she can be close to the old Kelvinator stove behind her (with one

dead plate in the front on the right) To serve up Roast chicken on Sundays After church

After he has changed out of his blue safari suit into his khaki shorts and his white

vest Roast chicken for lunch with thick dark gravy and crisp roast potatoes and mashed

beans and mashed pumpkin and white rice and nothing to drink Until afterwards

'Cause you'll fill yourself up, his father always says And you won't have space for

your mother's delicious food Fish fingers on Monday night with mashed potato and

thick dark gravy And mince on Tuesday with spaghetti and gem squash in their shells

And something else on Wednesday And Thursday And Friday And Saturday And

then Sunday again Roast chicken with thick dark gravy And afterwards rice pudding

or sago pudding or even, for special occasions like birthdays, a baked ginger pudding

And always with everything Custard Thick and yellow and hard From the blue and yellow

jug with a man in a blue suit and a pointed yellow hat as the handle And always

Springbok radio Consider Your Verdict The Money or the Box If I don't see you through

the week, I'll see you through the window And through the window he sees the

ghost of his brother with wide open eyes swimming up the long driveway that they

always raced their tricycles down and back up Racing each other to see who would

be first to get back to the garage and slap the cold roll-up door OneTwoThreeBlockMyself!

And he sees his brother's sad ghost Searching for him Like a hadeda with its long

beak Here There Everywhere No matter where he (the older one) goes Even when

he ends up at the Jan Richter Centre, Convalescent Home, Day Care, Frail Care, Assisted

Living, Any, on the corner of Walker Alley and New Scotland Road (No Hawkers

Allowed), behind a high palisade fence painted green And an

---

electronic motor-gate

with spikes on the top And a bored guard at the gate with his clipboard and his

tattered sheets of paper Where he (not the guard But this one The one at the heart

of this story With a hole in his heart) has a single room with a bed and a built-in cupboard

and a built-in desk in pressed chipboard with a plastic coating and a polished parquet

floor that is perilously slippery And a shower and a basin next door, and a bath and

a toilet in the middle of the long passage on every floor And on Sundays, in the big

dining hall that can accommodate two hundred and fifty residents sitting at rows of

steel trestle tables covered with red cloths that reach half-way to the ground, on Sundays

he has mince and mashed potatoes with boiled cabbage and carrots, and afterwards

for pudding, stewed fruit and Ultra Mel custard, vanilla flavoured And it is not No

It is not Not as if every single nerve and muscle and vein in his body is not growing

a skin over it Thick and cold as old custard From the blue and yellow jug with a

man in a blue suit and a pointed yellow hat as the handle.

The Room of Whiteness

Scraping.
Scraping. Up. Fragments.

There is

There it is again

The chair that sits in a small square room with damp walls and a dirty beige carpet

and a dim fluorescent light The chair that cannot do anything Anymore Go

anywhere Speak even Anymore The chair that sits in front of a louvred window

with its faded arms on either side and its thin legs closed and crossed at the feet

The chair that sits precisely where he always is Now And again And still On the

dusty carpet in the lounge at the feet of his sleeping father Playing with his green

plastic soldiers His little farm animals and little wooden blocks for building his

tower to the sky Pretending that something is happening Yes Anything That is

not the same as the thing that is happening the same all the time around him Now

Day in Day out Again Slowly Close-up In minute detail.

The Room of Absolute Whiteness

In handfuls.

There is

There is

a louvred window that faces straight onto a flat sky that runs left to right and back

again All day All night Even on public holidays When the wind is not there

The sky deserted Blood stalled in his little engine Just the small sounds of cooling

from the contraction of his muscles and his nerves and his brittle little bones

There is a louvred window that overlooks a car park (Residents Parking Only –

Vehicles Parked Entirely at Owner's Risk) (No Hawkers Allowed) A window that

is not able to remember anything Day in Day out From one moment to the next

The way the eyes of the dead forget forever everything they ever saw Or ever once remembered.

ACKNOWLEDGEMENTS

Special thanks to Andries Gouws for the use of his painting on the cover.

Thanks to Robert Berold for his commitment to publishing poetry and for his friendship.

The original version of *A Book of Rooms* was written as part of my 2010 doctoral thesis in Creative Writing at the University of KwaZulu-Natal, entitled *Autobiography of Bone*. My gratitude goes to my supervisors Michael Green and Michael Chapman.